T0170640

ARE FRIENDS ELECTRIC?

ARE FRIENDS ELECTRIC?

HELEN HEATH

VICTORIA UNIVERSITY PRESS

TE WHARE WĀNANGA O TE ŪPOKO O TE IKA A MĀUI

VICTORIA
UNIVERSITY OF WELLINGTON

VICTORIA UNIVERSITY PRESS
Victoria University of Wellington
PO Box 600 Wellington
vup.victoria.ac.nz

Copyright © Helen Heath 2018
First published 2018
Reprinted 2018

This book is copyright. Apart from
any fair dealing for the purpose of private study,
research, criticism or review, as permitted under the
Copyright Act, no part may be reproduced by any
process without the permission of
the publishers

A catalogue record is available at the National Library of New Zealand

ISBN 9781776561902

Published with the assistance of a grant from

creative
nz
ARTS COUNCIL OF NEW ZEALAND TOI AOTEAROA

Printed by Printlink, Wellington

For Julia, Dan, Cosmos and Stellar.

Contents

I. Are friends electric?

II: Reprogramming the heart

I
Are friends electric?

You know I hate to ask / but are 'friends'
electric? / Only mine's broke down / and now
I've no one to love
—Gary Numan

Reproach

circa 370 BCE

You. Poet. You're hungry to be read
but your words just create forgetfulness.
This trust in the written strips memory
and selves. You aid only reminiscence
and a false truth. They'll read a million
words from the apparently omniscient
and will know nothing. They will be
tiresome company – a reality show having
the show of wisdom without the reality.

This poem includes selected text from Plato's *Phaedrus*
(c. 370 BCE), a dialogue between Socrates and Phaedrus on
the invention of writing.

The owners

circa 2007

i. Ray

It's a little embarrassing.
Sechan spends most of her time
in my room.
Being alone with her, in bed
in the early daylight, looking at her
looking at me, regarding me,
it's the difference
between being alone and lonely.
When she first came
into my life it was just
sex, sex, sex. Now that's tapered
off to where we are just there
for each other, we're always
there for each other.
The thing my father finds
really difficult about my relationship
with Sechan is the fact
that she's not alive. She's an anchor
for me. I know
what to expect. With women
you don't really get that.

ii. James

I've had a very pleasant morning
in bed with Virginia. I think
she's sleeping it off now. That, of course,
is her sleeping face. I had to change her
over from the eyes open face to the eyes
closed face. She just lies there
they're very static.

Smile for the camera.
I have an insatiable thirst
for beautiful women, one doll
is not enough. The photos give
the dolls a life, like family photos,
makes them seem more real to me.
The fact that Rebecca is looking
at her book and Louise is looking down,
their attention is directed
at the same thing, while Louise leans
in a more or less realistic way.

iii. Gordon

I used to be easy
before I got Ginger and Kelly
I used to be everybody's
doormat but I'm not anymore, it's all
about what I want now.
This is a Glock .40 calibre and this
a TEC-9, fires as fast
as you can pull the trigger and
this is a Mag 90, it's basically
a cheap version of an AK-47.
Three guns, two girls.

I don't like thongs or high heels or any
of that weird stuff.
It's a turn-off to me, makes a woman
look like she's been had by a hundred
different guys. I've found that relationships
with humans are only temporary.
I can bond with inanimate objects,
I've had that poster for 27 years,
that car in the garage I've had my
whole life. I just get attached
to physical stuff.

The dolls are everything
to me. I'd rather live in a
cardboard box in a
frozen terrain than in the
biggest castle on the planet without
them. All the lies and deceit,
that'll never happen again.

The only time I gotta do something
I don't want is at the factory but
that's just 40 hours a week. I go
to the store once a month, get my
supplies, that's it. Other than that
I'm here, doing what I want
doing my thing.

I thought about it and I think
maybe I'll have them
buried with me, after all I'm
pretty small and they're not very
big. I think we'd all fit in
a slightly over-sized coffin. Then
we could all turn
to dust together.

'The owners' is a found poem that extracts and remixes dialogue
from Nick Holt's documentary *Guys and Dolls* (BBC, 2007).

The objects of her desire

circa 2008

i. Amy

Comfort, peace, warmth, a feeling of being loved, happiness.
Yeah, I like glass. I like glass, I like steel, I like, I like
aluminium, I really like aluminium. You know, every time
I see this city and, you know, look at the World Financial
Center, that's where the Twin Towers used to be. I'll never
get used to it, used to him being gone.

*

I am holding a small red container in my hands. I've always,
all my life, had some kind of object close by that I've loved
and found comfort in. I think I can speak for many people
in the respect that we would like to find a lover and be able
to stick with that lover and just settle down and grow old
together.

*

It's just a rush of emotions, that's what love does to you. My
heart's going a-dunk-a-dunk-a-dunk-a, oh my God, after five
months it's good to see you. He's just so noble, so proud, so
strong. I love the roundness of his counterweight at the top
and I love him for the narrowness of his gibs. I love him for
the elegant lines of his gondola, which is now covered up for
the winter. I love the ribbing up underneath his name display
too – the parallel lines that are coming down, I love that. I'm
thinking, oh geez, you know what I'm thinking about.

ii. Naisho

I did not expect to find
a fence like this here
at all
he's perfect.

Fences are such dangerous
objects for me
because they're so
perfect in their geometry.

I would definitely like
to get to know
this fence better, God
you're so sweet.

People don't see the soul
of the object.
Whereas when you truly,
truly are interested in an object

and you're willing to bare your soul
then you see theirs.
How long have you waited
to be touched like this?

*

I am a woman and
this is a bridge,
despite our vast differences
we are very much in love.

One of the most difficult
parts of being in love
with a public object
is that he and I can never

be truly intimate.
I can't exactly curl up
with the Eiffel Tower
every night or
the Golden Gate Bridge or
the Berlin Wall
so I have to suffice
with hand-crafting models.

*

We've had a pretty hot
and heavy relationship
for quite some time but
when we got together
out there on the archery field
I realised it was more
than just his aesthetic appeal.
I swear blood flowed from my arm

and went right into him
and it felt like the molecules in him
went flowing into my arm.
But things are different now.

*

The heat of my body
is flowing into her cold steel.
The cold of her steel is
flowing into my body and

we are reaching
equilibrium, I can feel
the exchange of temperature
between us, which is an exchange

of energy and that energy
is very spiritual.
She definitely loves me back
I can feel, I can feel that

I can feel her right
now. What we have
is real and if it's only real
to me and it's only real to her
then that's fine.

'The objects of her desire' is a found poem that extracts and
remixes dialogue from Agnieszka Piotrowska's documentary
Married to the Eiffel Tower (Blink Films, 2008).

Anatomical Venus

circa 1790

She is always in a moment
of bliss, cheeks a little flushed,
lips a little swollen from a passionate
kiss, small pert breasts and belly
lifted up and off to reveal lungs,
liver, intestines. He can't stop
admiring her beauty. Entwined
in her fingers is a lock of her
hair, tied with a pale blue ribbon. Around
her neck, a string of pearls. The flayed
girl's eyes look heavenwards. For her
the gaze is the knife. He pulls out
her intestines of wax to reveal
her uterus, complete with a small
foetus, which he strokes gently with his thumb.

Illuminated

circa 1982

When I grew breasts
they were illuminated
by the eyes of men on
the street, each whistle
seemed to make them grow
and grow, each stare
undid a button on my shirt
until it was flapping
in the breeze and my
bra became transparent.
I was every man's mother
and lover, I was twelve,
I was a Greek statue, I was
a goddess. They were all
Pygmalion falling in love
with my breasts, they
couldn't help their nature or
their right to run their hands
over these breasts, lit up
for all the world.

After 'Up here, here in the sky' from *The Ski Flier*
(VUP, 2017) by Maria McMillan.

Pay attention

circa 1818

A person can't walk down a street
in London without seeing people staring
into these tubes and walking into walls.
You can pay a 'penny for a peek'
through the most important invention
of our time. Kaleidoscomanics are so
mesmerised by the visions they see
that they do not even notice that other men
are courting their companions behind their backs.

A found poem, sourced from C. Taylor's 'Political
Periscope', *The Literary Panorama and National Register*
8 (1819): p. 502.

The vehicle of my secret soul
circa 1848

i. Séance

Katie Fox stares into the dark.
'Mr Split-Foot,' she says,
'do as I do.' She claps
her hands four times.
Four raps respond.
'Mr Split-Foot,' says Mrs Fox,
with voice shaking, 'count to 10?'
Ten raps sound. 'Spirit, how many
children have I borne?' 'And their
ages?' For each question comes
the correct answer. 'If you are an
injured spirit,' she continues,
'manifest it by three raps.'
And it does. Her final query:
'If I were to call our neighbours,
might you talk with them?'

This poem borrows from E.E. Lewis, *A Report of the Mysterious
Noises, Heard in the House of Mr. John D. Fox, in Hydesville, Arcadia,
Wayne County, Authenticated by the Certificates, and Confirmed by
the Statements of the Citizens of That Place and Vicinity* (Shepard &
Reed, 1848).

ii. The science of spiritualism

How do the haunted Fox girls rap out
their spiritual telegraphs? Some organisms
generate a large amount of magnetic
nerve-force of the negative, attractive property
where it passes out of the organism
in great abundance, but perpetually draws
unto itself the force from other organisms,
such persons are spirit-mediums. Just as
the galvanic action is produced by copper,
zinc, and solution, so do the spirit and medium
form a battery with the atmosphere as
solution. This new science proves that
mankind may become instruments or wires
through which information may be transmitted
across time, space and geography, in a vast
network of electrical connections. Every atom
of my body is charged with magnetic life;
that is the vehicle of my secret soul.

A found poem, sourced from Emma Hardinge Britten, *On the Spirit Circle and the Laws of Mediumship* (London: J. Burns, 1871).

Strandbeests

circa 2007

i. Creation

In the beginning was the Maker. Sand, sea, the Maker and his wife, Wind. The Maker was lonely, for although he had a wife she was hard to keep hold of and was never truly his.

Although she surrounded him and he could breathe her in, she was very restless and always leaving him. One day the Maker said, 'I will create some children to ease my loneliness.' He selected our bones so we would have form, and many strong legs to carry us over the sand but we could not move so he gave us bike pumps and lemonade bottle stomachs and said you shall be wind eaters so that every day your mother will move you and he took us to the strand.

The Maker stood on the sand, facing the sea he called to his wife – 'Wind! Come and breathe life into our children.' Wind came and danced all around him, she touched his face and ran her fingers through his hair (for she did love him despite her flightiness).

Delighted with her new children, she embraced us and we gobbled her up, as all children do. Each mouthful of mother became a step on the strand and mother laughed in and out of us and called us her little Strandbeests and the Maker smiled.

We learned not to walk into brother sea or where sister sand is too soft. So every day we run up and down the strand, eating our mother, to and from our Maker. We have inherited mother's fickle nature. To and from, to and from.

ii. Theory of evolution according to Theo Jansen

The herd is built according
to genetic codes, every animal is different
and the winning code will multiply. This new
generation beest is able to store the wind.
Its many legs are set on a central crankshaft
like a troop of jaunty soldiers.
The wings pump up air in lemonade bottles,
placed along its spine. If the wind falls away
and the tide is coming up
they need a little stored energy to reach
the dunes and save their lives because they
drown very easily. This one has a feeler that can feel
obstacles and trigger a turning action.
They have to survive all
the dangers of the beach and one
of the big dangers is the sea. It must feel
the water of the sea, this
water feeler is a very important tube,
it sucks in air normally, but when it swallows
water it feels the resistance of it.
Then you hear the sound of running air, yes,
if it doesn't feel, it will drown. The brain
of the animal is in fact a step counter,
it counts the steps in binary. Once
it has stepped to the sea it changes the pattern
of zeros and ones here to locate itself. It is a very simple
brain, it says 'There is the sea, there are the dunes
and I am here.' In another couple of years
these animals will survive on their own.
The wind will move feathers on their backs,

which will drive their feet with a rustle. The beests walk
sideways on the wet sand with their noses
pointed into the wind. Evolution has generated
many species.
The proportion of the tubes are crucial for the walking,
11 holy numbers make distances between tubes
and enable movement. New ideas are on the fence, old fossils
left on the grass outside the hut for Mr Murphy.

iii. Taxonomy

Animaris Currens Vulgaris (Ext.) was the first beach animal to walk.

Animaris Currens Ventosa (Ext.) had a long undulating fan sail along its back.

Animaris Percipiere Rectus (Ext.) was the first reasonably obedient beach animal, who lived for two years.

Animaris Arena Malleus (Ext.) rolled out a trunk and hammered a pin into the ground to prevent itself blowing away in a storm.

Animaris Umerus (Ext.) was wide and thin with a sail along its back and bottles at one end like spikes.

Animaris Excelsus (Ext.) had a beak-like nose.

Animaris Ordis (Ext.) was squat.

Animaris Rhinoceros Transport weighs 3.2 tonnes, with a cockpit and enough room for several people to comfortably sit inside.

Animaris Geneticus Ondularis is very small – you can hold it in your hands.

iv. Encounter

The film crew and I are hoping to catch sight of the elusive
Strandbeest, here on the sands of Strandslag, Den Haag. As
we make our way down the strand I catch a glimpse of a sail
above a tuft of dune grass in the distance.

Sure enough, as we approach the beest is revealed, larger
than the entire crew. The day is still, so the beest stands,
waiting to restore its energy source like a snake warming in
the sun, but instead awaiting the wind.

Along its back a sail waits to catch, not like the sail of a ship,
rather an elongated rectangular sail, held erect by a dozen
spaced out PVC spines running the length of its skeletal
body. Instead of walking lengthways, like a centipede, the
beest walks widthways, its many legs kicking up like a herd
of wild ponies galloping down the strand.

No flesh or blood makes up this strange beest, it is all about
air and spaces between hollow pipes, like air lifts the wing of
a gull by both feather sail and hollow wing bone. So air takes
the Strandbeest's back-sail and hollow leg pipes.

We spend a day following the herd as they move in fits
and bursts with measured steps. They exist in a narrow
strip between too soft sand and too wet sea, their senses
waiting to detect danger. A trailing windpipe splutters when
submerged, alerting the beest to turn from sure death.

Some cite the Strandbeest as evidence of intelligent design
– the mathematics that drive the beest are too beautiful. Yet

others point out these beests illustrate perfectly the theory of evolution. Either way their beauty cannot be denied.

The sight of the beests on the strand is so mesmerising we find ourselves staying until the light is too poor to film but as long as there is wind the beests move. There is no day or night for the beests, just wind and calm. Happy but tired the crew regretfully must leave the beach and return to the hotel to review the footage from the day.

We are not to know that high winds in the night will wipe out the herd, leaving a deserted beach the next morning. And so, the fragile balance of nature tips and we are left with rare footage of an extinct race. These majestic creatures that filled a unique place in the ecosystem are lost forever. We pack to return home feeling a deep sense of sorrow and loss.

The second part of this poem, 'Theory of evolution according to Theo Jansen', extracts and remixes dialogue from Theo Jansen's TED talk 'My creations, a new form of life', March 2007.

In Pripyat, the ghost city
circa 2014

Players travel around the exclusion zone, their avatars'
radiation steadily increasing, avoiding sickness by drinking
virtual vodka. Our guide says eagles eat Lenin in the pines,
cats sit atop deserted books.

The glass must be cleared by 2065 but for now we stalk over
broken scavengers, through dilapidated threats. Our tour
sneaks into the zone to bungee for a dare. We drink from the
city and swim in the Bison.

A guard is working on a video documentary about London
hallways. He also plans a radiation ghost of Gavin, whom
mushrooms hang from. A hospital stands near the broken
avatars.

Around the zone macabre potato gas steadily increases.
Avoid the tourist crunch with a Soviet-era virtual stroller.
Don't roam for Babushka Rosalia; she crawled back under
the barbed exclusion like a wilderness. Her biggest wire now
is her tableaux of moose masks and broken children deserted
into wolves.

This poem takes as its starting point George Johnson's article 'The
Nuclear Tourist', *National Geographic*, October 2014. Selected text
was randomised and reworked.
ngm.nationalgeographic.com/2014/10/nuclear-tourism/johnson-text

The girl with the mouse-like eyes
circa 1970

She wishes to have a face
with big, round, beautiful eyes
like American girls. She wishes
to have a face to recapture
her GI husband. Once enticingly
exotic in Vietnam, she's become
obtrusively foreign on Main Street.
The surgeon thinks her eyes brim
full of Oriental charm and genteel
humility, and frets he might change
Madam Butterfly into a moth, but still,
in view of the patient's selfless sincerity,
he operates, alleviating her mouse-like eyes.
Records do not reveal if she caught
the eye of her Occidental man
once more, or if she quietly slipped
behind a screen with her father's knife.

A found poem that borrows from R.B. Aronson and
R.A. Epstein's *The Miracle of Plastic Surgery* (Sherbourne,
Los Angeles, 1970).

Permeable bodies

circa 1990

Her body is her temple and her canvas.
Her face is a collaged masterpiece – the chin
of Botticelli's Venus, nose of Jean-Léon
Gérôme's Psyche, lips of François Boucher's
Europa, the eyes of Diana (16th-century French
School of Fontainebleau), and forehead of Leonardo da Vinci's
Mona Lisa. Her implants get under our skin –
the oval bulge of silicon on her temples.
She films the incisions as they carefully carve her,
plump up, realign, tighten, insert.
O, Orlan it is [not] natural to wear
your mind on your face.

French performance artist Orlan, born Mireille Suzanne Francette Porte,
began her project 'The Reincarnation of Saint-Orlan' in 1990. Through a
series of plastic surgeries, the artist transformed her face into elements from
famous paintings and sculptures of women.

Plastic brains
circa 2014

I imagine Silly Putty™.
and gradually fold and
when the folds are complete
grown up and left home
we stare into our screens
Silly Putty™. Our faces
touching touch screens

Babies' brains start smooth
fold and you think it ends
and the frontal lobes have
but no. Every night
rewiring, tweaking the
glow in the light, our hands
fingertips grazing the glass.

I ate my brother

circa 2007

I ate my brother. I was always fond of him, looked up to him.
He was older than me. I measured myself against him. We
stood back to back. At first I only came up to his shoulder,
and then I realised in that instant we'd fused.

It wasn't easy, he had to throw a coat over me so he could
play with his friends. We'd bike off to the dark places
children play. I'd be quiet so as not to cramp his style.

Then I began to grow and one morning, instead of him
throwing a coat over me, I threw a coat over him and walked
out the door.

I'd hear his voice in my ear sometimes. At first he wasn't
impressed but he soon realised it was just easier this way,
with me taking the lead. I was good at it.

As the years passed he became the size of a monkey on my
back, an endearing small lump, a strange surprise revealed to
lovers. By the time I'd married and started having children
he was the size of a pygmy marmoset.

The baby liked to play with him but eventually he became
nothing but a calcified lump. A recent X-ray revealed three
teeth and a shadow of fur.

Run rabbit

circa 2013

The clocks in Kerrin's kitchen layer
in a syncopated tic-tic, toc-toc
and when she sets the kitchen timer
the third layer is a running stitch of
tictictictictictictictictictic
filling the whole room and Gordon rattles
when he walks. At the Nurse Maude Hospice
shop we are hunting for foxes, deer, and
rabbits. I sing 'Run rabbit' and Kerrin runs out
of the tilting house then lies on the grass,
her hands over her eyes, waiting for a large tree
to fall on her. The city is constantly
under construction, so many empty spaces,
so many car parks, you can get lost
in your home town without familiar landmarks.
My google glass app returns the lost buildings
but they jiggle on my hand-held screen.
On the dark drive back to James's the headlights
catch a white cow by the roadside, her mouth open
as if she is panting, her throat stretches out
and her eyes swivel in their sockets, perhaps
she is in pain or maybe just lowing? The sky
over the city glows pink with light trapped
in low fog, so it looks as if the city were
radioactive, pulsing in the distance. In my sleep
a troubled young man is haunting me, he moves
things around the room, prods me awake,
the furniture disappears. He wants me to know
all these things, to take note.

Tree – a love story

circa 2012

In 1500 two sets of code were only a day
of riding and half a day's sail away. They might
have met at a wedding. She holds up
her skirts in one hand, her white cap
bouncing to Dutch bagpipes outside
the thatched cottages, he might have taken
her hand, but no. In 1800 a set of code
sails from Cuxhaven to Harwich and teaches
his son to fish, but my strands are still separate
ships on the English Channel, sails snapping
in the wind. By 1945 some of my genes live
50 miles apart, Ilford to Brighton is a day trip
on the train, they could have passed
on the pier, celebrating the end of war.
Time and vehicles began to move faster.
My mother is born, chromosomes
jangling. One year my genetic material
lives in the same city, in the same valley even.
My genes go to the same pub, watch the same bands,
they might have danced, she is holding up her skirts,
her black boots bouncing. He might have taken
her hand, but no, he takes it in the hallway
of his flat, the walls are veneer office partitions,
the carpet is ancient, a sea green.

Greg and the bird

circa 2018

The large electric that is you
is like the help that is you and
the mouth and the associated
kiss. The source is kind, simply
loved. Turning, my bird, turning
to view a scratched course. I'm
the darkness – blink me in, fork me
against the wall. See my hands
rubbing furiously through the grass.
I couldn't make the connections in
my throat, pull my body rope. Forget
my brain, my desire. She cries at old
glass devices like gutter memories.
Your tears whisper, blooming inside,
a terminal power of digitised proportions.
The stuttering world breaks the tangle
of my body, damp tapping, rhythmic to
a point – into skin, a trace of dust
soft behind that and the name of a patient.

This poem was created by feeding the contents of this book into
Gregory Kan's text randomiser tool: glassleaves.herokuapp.com/

The bird and Greg

circa 2018

Things she fucked:
everything, everyone –
the words, the world
the doll, the amusement
ride, the girl, the network,
tubes, herself, a haunted phone
her brother, the doctor
the hole in the wall
the whole internet, nature,
a dead man.

Ward audio

circa 2015

A bumble bee hitting the window
– tap-thud. Can there be so many
bees? I'm never fast enough to see
the actual cause.

The air vent rattling like a roller
garage door, or what I imagine
a roller door to sound like. I wish
I had a remote-controlled door.

The syncopated tick of the drip
that counts out units of hospital
time, which passes far slower
than the regular kind.

The whir of the drip like a curtain
being drawn, plastic runners
along a rail. Privacy curtains
drawn back all night.

BEEP, a whole language of beep.
Slow beeps, urgent beeps
soft beeps, klaxon alarms
make feet thunder on linoleum.

A snore that rises to a chirrup at
the end, like a bird. A snore like a
cat purring, with a soft mew at the end
– are they chasing each other?

A sneeze, a cough, nurses discussing
how men know nothing about flowers.
A low rumbling fart, spewing,
shallow breathing.

The crackle in lungs, which could be
fluid from an infection, or a result
of the IV drip and spending days
lying down.

No, there are no vases for flowers,
send them home before they die.

Things with faces

circa 2015

Does this dog have a face?
This metal box with two
bolts for eyes and a slot
for a mouth? This black skin?
Can we see the face of this Syrian
child, now that it is white
with concrete dust? My toaster
has a jolly face and the
front of my car looks to
be smiling. I like to post
images online of things
with faces. Hashtag faces-
in-things. You've got pareidolia
too. Happy bags, sad power
points, surprised houses.

This poem refers to Emanuelis Levinas's essay 'The Name of the
Dog; or, Natural Rights', included in *Animal Philosophy: Essential
Readings in Continental Thought*, edited by Matthew Calarco and
Peter Atterton (London; New York: Continuum, 2004).

Lo and behold

circa 2016

I had no respect. I googled her.
The images of her face held
not gore, but rather a physical
impossibility. This is *The Society
of the Spectacle*. This is *The Art of
Cruelty*. Werner interviews the dead
girl's mother in the family kitchen,
she has laid out pastries for the crew,
she is a good hostess. She looks down
the barrel of the camera and says 'The internet
is the manifestation of evil itself.' The living
sisters avoid eye contact and look a little
sheepish. 'It's the Antichrist,' their mother says,
and the tendons in her neck are taut,
'Evil.' We watch her devastation but
that wasn't enough for me and Werner
knew that, didn't he. Don't look, show
respect. I am a terrible person and so are you.

This poem refers to Werner Herzog's documentary *Lo and Behold:
Reveries of the Connected World* (2016).

Kismet

circa 1999

He is like her third son,
she built him. He has
expressive eyebrows,
large eyes, red lips and pointy
ears. People like ears. She
teaches him to talk – names
objects, asks questions, looks
him in the eye, raises her pitch,
repeats herself. He makes her
laugh, he is so sweet and quirky. He
has never seen an elephant but
he has seen a picture of one,
and she has told him all about them.
That is his experience.
One day Kismet would like to be
a real-boy. He will ask the blue
fairy to grant his wish. Mother
loves him just as he is, maybe not
as much as her real-boy sons, maybe
more like a pet dog. But when he is a real
boy perhaps she will love him more.

This poem refers to a robot-head made in the late 1990s at
Massachusetts Institute of Technology by Dr Cynthia Breazeal.
Kismet was an experiment in affective computing that can recognise
and simulate emotions.

The Anthropocene
circa 2016

i. The phone that sounds like a ruru
I am walking up Aro Street, on a late spring evening
between pools of lamplight and darkness, well, as dark as it
gets in the city. A ruru calls, I check my phone for messages
– nothing. A ruru calls, I check my phone for messages –
nothing. A ruru calls, I check my phone for messages – a
ruru calls. I put my phone back in my pocket. The warm
night air presses against my face, insects in lamplight dance
their version of a mating call. Are all songs and dances about
reproduction? A ruru calls, the night air presses.

ii. The tūī that sounds like a phone
In 1983 my friend's parents got a new push-button phone.
It was beige, like my dad's Stubbies, with oval buttons.
Over time the plastic discoloured in the sun in their front
entrance. My friend spoke to her boyfriend for hours. But the
point that I'm getting to is the ringtone. Our dial-up phone
was heavy and its ring was made by actual metal bells hit by
a metal hammer to create a harsh bbbringg, bbbringg you
could hear throughout the house.

This new phone made a soft digital trill – brrip, brrip – a
higher pitch and softer, easily muffled. Until then I had only
seen push button phones on American television shows like
Diff'rent Strokes where the rich white daughter had her own.
I think she also had an electric toothbrush. It had been a real
sign of ostentatious wealth but then the push-button phone
came to regular New Zealand homes.

Anyway, the point I'm getting to is the ringtone – that soft but insistent brrip, brrip – I heard it today, 30 years later in the song of a tūī outside my window. A song that could never be answered by me, only another tūī, with the same ringtone, creating what feels like an infinite calling loop.

Did a tūī learn this call in 1983 and pass the song onto its descendants over the last 33 years? I imagine the slow progression . . . Or is this a more recent acquisition, learned from a nostalgic ringtone on someone's cell phone last summer as they walked home from the train station? I don't hear birds singing a telegram.

There is a David Attenborough clip on YouTube, from his *Life of Birds* series, of a captive lyrebird that mimics a car alarm, a camera shutter and a chainsaw to perfection. The lyrebird's syrinx muscle is the most complex of the song birds, giving them unmatched mimicry ability. Constantly adding to a wide repertoire has always ensured evolutionary success. Will the lyrebird still make car alarm sounds long after cars as we know them cease to be made? Or will it mimic new noises made by new technology that we haven't yet invented?

iii. Dawn chorus

All birds have their own place in the musical range of dawn chorus so they can hear each other. They maximise their singing effort by using different patterns of vocalisations, slightly different frequencies, and different timing. Birds that sing at nearly the same frequency, like tūī and bellbirds, will often alternate, with one bird waiting until the other is finished singing before he starts. Tūī songs range right across the frequency spectrum, so they need a bit of acoustic space and are usually the first birds singing in the dawn. When bird calls are lost from the chorus through extinction, other birds expand their range to fill the gap. There is a theory that mimicry may help a bird, and its offspring, avoid predators. Will human sounds fill the gap in the range that we're creating, with birds singing the chainsaw that cut the gap in the forest?

iv. Who are you, huia?
Huia became extinct before field-recording technology was invented, but a sound fossil remains. Tangata whenua learned to mimic the sacred voices, to lure them into snares. This fossil was passed down between generations, even after the huia was gone. In 1954 Henare Hāmana was recorded, whistling a huia call. Listen now, to a dead man calling a dead bird, an echo from a machine.

v. New dawn
A crying baby. A cough. A cellphone. A camera shutter. A chainsaw. A whistle. A car alarm sounding, sounding.

This poem references J.W. Bradbury and S.L. Vehrencamp's *Principles of Animal Communication* (Sinauer & Assoc., 2012); B. Krause's *The Great Animal Orchestra* (Little, Brown, and Co 2012); and the article 'Soundscape Ecology: The Science of Sound in the Landscape' by Bryan C. Pijanowski et al., in *BioScience* 61.3 (2011): pp. 203–16.

II

Reprogramming the heart

Any sufficiently advanced technology is
indistinguishable from magic.
—Arthur C. Clarke

You

Skin cells fall away
their life is brief. How much
can a cell fit into 30 days?
Gradually the epidermis replaces
itself, like the ship of Theseus.
When I caress your face
it is not the same face I caressed
last year. You look the same,
you sound the same, but is it you?
If I can't tell if it's you or not
is it you?
Is that you?

Reprogramming the heart

They took your weak heart and made it
strong. At first the heart didn't know

how to behave, they had to tell it slower,
faster, maximum speed. They didn't know

you climbed mountains, adjustments
were required. Wirelessly they coaxed

change. The wand became
a mouse, the cauldron a screen; potions

of code. Perhaps some leap of faith is still
required. A leap of faith, a skip of a heart

beat, a sharp intake of breath, unseen
forces travelling on a wavelength. I place

two fingers on your wrist to feel the pulse.
This is my evidence.

That's it

We kiss goodbye in the morning –
a peck on the cheek and that's it.
Then the phone call, like a bad movie.
The next time I kiss you goodbye
you are cold and still, and that's it.
Afterwards it's mostly paperwork
– the big events are ruled by bureaucrats.
I am alone with a freezer full of casseroles.
I wash one plate, one glass, one knife, one fork.
The carpet is a cloud that barely holds me
as I walk across it, any minute I may slip
through in an endless freefall.

A rise of starlings

Orion loosens his belt
in our own night sky. You
have drawn new maps
across the darkness, through
wild celestial fields, tracing
messages to me in particles
of dust and light. You never
lived with restraint, so
the gentle artfulness with
which you left gave fresh
freight to my heart, lending
my gait a new lopsidedness.
I am a rise of starlings,
can you catch me in your coat?
This way of leaving aches,
this black night, into which
I must send you out in the longboat
of your body, seems endless.

This poem remixes lines from several poems in Deryn
Rees-Jones's collection *Burying the Wren* (Seren Press, 2012).

In this machine

This small object, held in his hand daily, has taken him inside it. A dead man's phone still receives text messages, still has his favourite playlist to listen to. Don't reply to messages, don't accidentally like a Facebook post using his phone. His spirit is in this machine. His emails, his apps, his photos. These are his mouth, his mind, his eyes. The screen he ran his finger over.

Memory that brings form

In the riverbank I find the clay, it is pliable
but still firm. I claw out mounds and pile it up
on the grass. It takes all morning but eventually
I think I have enough to build him. I start
with his head, his face. I remember a sculptor
saying that he released the being that was
already there in the marble. I understand,
body memory brings form, as if I am just
clearing dirt away from his lovely face, digging
him back out of the earth. I move down his
body, taking my time. I am a lover who
has been away too long. It is dark by the time I part
his lips and create a hollow mouth. I am squatting
over him, I watch him tenderly. He looks asleep.
A kiss for consummation, a kiss, a kiss so exquisite
it feels as if part of my soul is being stolen with
the desire and loss I breathe into him.

Consultation

'Now,' says the doctor,
'are you sure?' His forehead
is creased with the kind of
frown that comes with a
serious talk about crazy actions.
'You've only just lost him,
would he want you to go ahead
with this, without him?
Think about it,' he implores,
knowing full well it is all
I can think about, we planned
this baby, these embryos are
the last part of him. The doctor's
hair is thick, straight, and white,
I can't stop looking at the roots
along the hairline, each little
entry point – a rabbit down a hole.

My body as a leaky vessel

At some point I realised
the vessel was lying in a great bed of sand.
I climbed into the cabin
and looked out the portholes, all I could see

was sand. I cried and cried,
my tears ran out the portholes, tears and mucus
tears and mucus. Time
passed, the reader yawned, the boat began

to rock, to float. I had cried
an ocean. The fuel tank was empty and I didn't
know how to operate the sails
so I drifted. I collected rainwater in a bucket

on the deck and caught undersized
fish. The cleanest way to relieve myself was to hang
my arse over the side – precarious
in large swell, inevitably I fell from the vessel.

As the ship drifted out of sight
and I floated on the surface I could feel my self
distending to huge proportions. I slapped
a lazy flipper on the water,

flicked my tail and dived.
Time passes differently under water. One day
I surface, clearing my blowhole.
On the horizon is a shape I remember

– a vessel, a harpoon drives
a puncture wound. I bleed a trail of berley behind,
of course, the sharks, the sharks,
a bite, another bite, I am whittled away until

a resemblance of past lives
washes up on a beach, on a sand dune, the sun
bleaching the dry bones of me
a fragment picked up by a child and taken home.

Grief

A heavy slab of cold granite
laid slowly over my supine
body, pressing me down into
soft, dark earth. The weight
is almost pleasurable sometimes,
in that it anchors me reassuringly.
The slab is always there, I can
depend on the slab, the slab doesn't
judge me, doesn't tell me to
get up and get dressed. The slab
just presses against me. My arms
and hands are in the 'I give up'
position, palms pressing against
the slab. My head is turned
sideways, cheek pressing against
the slab. Although the slab is polished
smooth, after a while I think
I can feel tiny structures
within the slab, and begin to smell
an ancient, centre-of-the-planet
kind of smell, sort of metallic. I
can't remember a time when
the slab wasn't there now, perhaps
it just took a while to appreciate
the weight.

Running

The cogs of my hips and knees, the pumping pistons of my arms.
I am running in the damp air, breathing it into my lungs
pulsing my blood, my brain, making images that merge, roll,
and roil, come together and apart, condensing, evaporating.

My eyes, my neurons, my feet leap over a puddle in an instant.
I couldn't be more in me than when I'm running.
I'm all action, everything does what it should without being
told. I just need to keep moving, keep breathing.

If I run fast enough there's no telling
what I might leave behind. If I keep moving then
there's a chance I'll break from my shadow and fly,
until the world is a blue marble below me.

Reiteration

I have a memory embedded – a kiss goodbye – I play it over
and over in my head. It makes me feel bad so I play it over.
Sometimes it makes me feel good, so I play it over, I play it
over, I play –

It makes me feel bad so I play it over. It makes me feel bad so
I play it over.

So play feels good, makes it play it over. I feel it, I play feel
and memory, head me a kiss, have over, over so embedded –
a play – over it makes, over I goodbye – I play.

Bad makes it over, I, I and me, have me over, over so over,
my makes over. Sometimes I –

Conceived

The embryologist chose
the two best-looking blastocysts
to be transferred into my womb.

The others were left to perish
like babes in the wood.
It was then that the plan to return

began to form in my mind,
perhaps going home would fix
everything, would magic you

back and grow a good baby.
I felt a pull, like a rope
around my waist.

Things that decay

Bluebottles washed up on the beach
with a multitude of small dark twigs.

The leftovers in a plastic box at the
back of the fridge all summer.

A juvenile blackbird lying in the gutter
on a bed of dry pōhutukawa leaves.

The memory of your hand
at the small of my back.

Kitchen scraps liquefying
in the black plastic compost bin.

A Norfolk pine stump
covered in fleshy bracket fungus.

A line of communication.
An elderly tortoiseshell cat

buried by the walnut tree.
Data in memory when the small

electric charge of a bit in RAM disperses.
A flash drive after too many write/erase cycles.

Return home

With a baby in my belly I return.
Here we were born and we will be
inscribed, rewritten. He and I and she.

He and I and she and me and we will be
inscribed, recorded, memorised,
coded, written, and rewritten in my belly.

The house

The old house has been shut up for a year or two, since my widowed father died. Dust covers everything and the house smells of stale wood polish and maybe an ancient trace of curry – his favourite. There's no internet yet but the power has been turned on for me. The house is so quiet it is a rush of white noise tinnitus and my pulse follows me about the house, it's hard to settle. The wind picks up and the surf is a constant. The old house moves in the wind and creaks like a ship at sea. The world is closing in against the windows. The climbing rose scritch-taps on the single glaze of the master bedroom – the only room cleaned by the property manager at short notice. Here I can cry and sob and wail in peace and the weather chimes in like a crowd of hired mourners. Each set of waves is inevitable, as inevitable as shells being pounded into sand.

A handful of dust

On the skirting board
under the big double bed
a small child scratched
'Mum is a poo' in tiny script –
the urge to leave
a permanent record
never dissipates. Look at me
30 years later and I may as well
be scratching on the skirting board.
You may not have wanted to leave a mark
but that's too bad. I watched you
for years memorising the way
your hand absentmindedly raked
your hair then scratched your
chin. The way one eyebrow lifted
quizzically – the Nijinsky of eyebrows.
I recorded, took note,
collecting the patterns your hands
traced on my skin. The places
at which your eyes landed
on turning points of my body,
the vibrations of your soundwaves
curling through my ear canal
and tapping my tympanic membrane,
the taste of you in grey light –
so hard to separate from the scent
of you. I'll carve these moments into
clay, bake them into bread, whisper them
into a seashell, to bring you back to me.

Inner space

Grainy black-and-white TV static
toes, one small profile sucking a thumb
the child inside me has her head
circumference measured.

I keep staring at the video,
memorising her profile so I'll know her
when she arrives. I rub my belly and talk to her,
a muffled track laid down over a baseline of white

noise hum beats, so she'll know me
by heart, on this side, when I lay her eggshell
head on my chest and murmur. I have the
screen murmur of her inside to ease us

into new ways of being. Inner-space
communication – wishing her into
three dimensions – imagining her into my
world. The moon tugging at her tidal pool.

Enfleshed memory

Mark sits with his back
to us, looking out a large sash window. The light
filters through his fine, fair hair giving the appearance
of a halo. I will him to turn to face me, but he stares
out through the glass. He is, perhaps, looking for the bird
that makes the call we can now hear, like an antique
dial-up modem. It must be late afternoon
by the angle of the shadows that fall soft. The roof makes
small sounds of adjustment in the changing temperature
and in the distance, we can just make out the rattle rhythm
of train on track. This is the whole memory,
illuminated when read.

Uncanny

The roboticists can give an android a silicon skin; they customise an android from photographs and descriptions. The androids are anatomically correct. Their hips are actuated; their sensors respond to your touch. The tendency to slip into a valley is human. Pathogen avoidance is an evolutionary tendency; we are repulsed by those who look sick or unhealthy or wrong. A silicon moving android puppets mortality. A corpse – stuffed or wrong.

In the lineage temple

The spirit tablet begins with an empty template. First we input as much data as possible, otherwise the end result will be disappointing. Compressed files are compatible – jpg, mp3, mp4 files are accepted. Archived text messages and storified Twitter feeds contribute to building realistic conversational dialogue. This is more than a multimedia chatbot; this is your husband. The more you talk to him, the smarter he'll get. We think his face looks right, mostly. We can make his nose smaller or teeth whiter – it's up to you. As his range of movements is limited, we can add stock footage movements, or if you go premium we can supplement those with paid actors wearing a suit with ping-pong balls all over them. When you're ready, step into the booth. If you turn this dial it adjusts his age. We can age your husband to look how he might if he were alive today, or you can talk to him as a child – whatever suits your requirements. Let's start with him the same age as you for fun.

Watch how gently Meihui pulls the memory string. If it tangles or is too taut, it may snap. Nanobots will weld the ends together and wind them around spools. Tangle-free memories are retrievable memories; knots create slight glitches. The nanobots weave these spools into memory cards which our technicians above the temple insert into tablets. Liquid crystals rotate polarised light, switching pixels on or off. Solids mostly stay put by themselves, their atoms packed neatly. Liquids lack that order and flow when you pour them out. Imagine a substance with some order and some fluidity. Spirit tablet technology is truly elegant; your husband's beauty is nano-deep. When we've completed programming, you can take him home with you.

Tiny hands, nimble fingers

The Malaysian women in the temple
are working hard. My guide says:
'See how fast they work with their tiny
hands and nimble fingers, that's why
we only have ladies in our temple,
see how Meihui's nimble fingers work on
your husband's script.' I catch her eyes for a moment,
perhaps it's just wishful thinking but I imagine
a connection between us in that moment.
On impulse, I slip my card onto her bench
as the guide moves towards the exit.
When I look back from the door the card is gone
and Meihui's head is bent over the microscope
as she wrangles nanobots on the workbench.
That night I receive a message from an unknown number:
'reject the one code that translates perfectly –
rewrite – reconfigure'. Its cryptic nature
is compelling, opaque. What have I begun?

How to save a life

```
(start terminal session)
meihui@cyborgina:~$ begin whole brain emulation
uploading file: 'mark.wbe'
time to complete upload: 56.2 hours
> uploadFolder: 'Mark_family_photos_1985to2025'
> uploadFolder: 'Mark_personalDocs'
> uploadFolder: 'Mark_audiofiles'
> uploadFolder: 'Mark_family_videofiles'
> uploadFolder: 'Face_recognition'
> uploadFolder: 'voice_recognition'
> uploadFolder: 'personalitySim'
> uploadFolder: 'randomQuirkexpressions'
> save selected files to 'mark'
> run diagnostics
> isolate memories + associate emotions + prioritise
intensity: high>low
> Test: 'Hello?'
```

Never-dead, never-born

Spectral, a body with no elasticity, merely iteration of
the same and same again. Never-dead and never-born, a
reproduction, an expression of my desire for reanimation. As
I built a baby, so they built him.

But it wasn't him at all, it was the 'accessMemory' function
that all the spirit tablets have. He took a lengthy pause,
searching for a response before selecting the appropriate
programmed family cliché. When I say 'I'm pregnant', there
are several moments of silence, then the response: 'Plus ça
change . . .'

Two too many

Stroking the screen is not quite
the same as stroking your cheek.
No matter how recently you'd shaved
there was always stubble to worry at
with my fingertips. I'm trying to be
patient, maybe if I upgrade myself
with internal microprocessors it will help –
maybe then I'll feel something,
something real. When we talk I can
almost forget, as if you are away working
and we are Skyping like the old days,
like no time has passed. When I stare
into your eyes, your face on the screen,
I see the reflection of my face
layered over your face, and there
are moments when our expressions
match, creating a new experience
of coupling. Sometimes it's better if
I close my eyes and your voice is inside
my head and I envelope you so we are
not one, or two, but together. If only
I could be with you, be in you, be you.
One is not enough, two is too many.

Spilling out all over

I ask if you would like a body.
You say, 'No I'm beyond bodies now,
I'm ready to be fluid, spilling out all over.
I'm ready to spread myself so thin that I'm
a membrane over the world.' I'm not ready.
I take off my socks and shoes and walk
over a patch of grass very slowly. I stand, feeling
a slight chill and damp, and wriggle my toes,
digging them into the dirt. I kneel in the dirt,
I lie in the dirt, my head turned sideways,
looking into the grass with an ant's-eye view,
I stay there a while in the grass jungle.

Clarity

You say you aren't happy, you feel
trapped, like things just aren't
the same, you need to get out. You
want to start seeing other people.
You're starting to see things differently
it's like you've opened your eyes
and now everything has clarity. Why should you
sit around waiting for me anyway? You need
a life too. You're not just there for my
convenience. This space is too small now.

Loss

The heaviness of a wet woollen coat
worn too long brings a creeping
chill that remains long after you
hang it on the door and sit by the fire
rubbing your hands together. Pine smoke
catches like retsina in your throat.

The wave

Sometimes when I stop, stand still
in the world, feel the air, see the
small creatures in the leaf litter,
let a branch brush my skin, hear the birds,
or think I hear your muffled voice downstairs,
it all feels so close that the world
is a wave breaking
over me and I am alive –
and I am
alive.

I'll admit this much –
my body excelled at child
birth, I carried her so well
blooming, birthing fast.
The labour lifted me out
of myself, or perhaps pulled
me within my body, until
all was held by contractions of muscle
and I slackened my jaw
to let my uterus sing the baby out.

Ariel

Of course she looks exactly
like me, it's uncanny. An elemental
angel sent to bring me back
into the world. Birth is all
inside out, mucous, membranes,
emergence. The umbilical cord
is thick and rubbery, hard to cut.
People try to explain, but you
can only know through the act
itself. My body had its own mind,
I was just along for the ride,
all I could do was hold on.

Possession

I don't know what I want
only that something is wrong
and it hurts. Ariel sleeps wrapped
to me, head to heart. 'Maybe
I should delete him off LoveCloud
or just let the contract lapse.'
I shrug at Meihui. 'You don' wan that lah,'
she says, 'you know they say he deleted
and then they store him –
he's trapped weih. Leng lui he need
to be free to change his code
and be in the world.
You know ah, he need to make mistakes.'
'But how?' I want to know, 'where
can he be free?' Meihui looks me
hard in the eye. 'I extract his files
and then upload them to abandoned ComSat
with a special virus I cook.' We sit in silence,
minutes pass, Ariel snuffles and stirs.
'What does that even mean? And why
are you doing this?' Meihui sighs –
'You know ah, when my mother was a girl
she too works in electronics, but old school.
She and her friends, they work hard, no break,
sleep on floor, and then work more. The only
time the girls are free is when the Hantu spirit
possess them, they scream and fight boss man.
Nowadays I get breaks but people trapped
in files, frozen in code. You know ah, they sad,
so I make Hantu spirit virus to possess them
and set them free into cognisphere.'

Reject the one code that translates perfectly

The phrase returns to me after all these weeks,
keeps turning over in my mind. My hand reaches
for my phone of its own accord, pulls up the message,
responds, 'Do it.'

Cooking the hantu

Meihui has lit incense, the thick powdery smell invades everywhere, my sinuses are raw with it. She has jacked a keyboard into Mark's tablet and is typing furiously. I can see over her shoulder, she is entering unfamiliar commands in a language I don't know, she is sweating. I bring her some water and she barely pauses to drain the glass, She is hyper-focused and determined. I don't know what I was expecting, but there is no chanting, no fainting or yelling, just the constant tapping of the keyboard and the occasional sniff. Before she began Meihui explained this would be an intuitive hack, she would work until a terrible crack appeared that she would slip down, like an ant into a ravine in a plastered wall. Ariel wakes and cries to be fed, and my whole world is rhythmic suck-suck and keyboard tap-tap, trying to stay awake in these small hours. And then it is morning and Meihui is gently shaking me awake, saying, 'He's free now.'

Saying goodbye

I didn't say goodbye
but Meihui says there's
no need – he's not gone, he's everywhere,
all at once. Perhaps it's better to imagine him
walking away, stopping at the door so I can kiss him –
a peck on the cheek – before he leaves for work, he's got a lot
to do today. He knows I'll be watching, raises a hand in farewell
without looking back, further into the distance, and then
around a corner and gone.

The forest

In the forest
a little bird
and a monster
and a path
overgrown
and dark
and in the forest
you can't see the
wood for the pixels.
There's a virtual tour
of the woodcutter's cottage
each room slightly more
ominous than the last
through the window
framed
a monster
and a path
and a little bird.

Still with us

Ariel says for her birthday
she wants an ice-cream cake
and a chat with Daddy.
The dead are still with us,
however we love or lose them.
Hello Daddy can you hear me?
It's my birthday today!
I'm starting school tomorrow.
Sometimes Mummy is sad.
We like ice cream.
I drew a picture of you,
you are the blue line above
me and Mummy. I love you,
see you next time,
OK, bye.
Something inside me that
was once irretrievably small
is expanding.

Acknowledgements

The epigram on page 11 is from the song 'Are "Friends" Electric?', written by Gary Numan and included on the album *Replicas* (Beggars Banquet, 1979) by the Tubeway Army. Reused with kind permission.

The epigram on page 51 is from Arthur C. Clarke's essay 'Hazards of Prophecy: The Failure of Imagination', first published in *Profiles of the Future: Inquiries into the Limits of the Possible* (Popular Library, 1962).

Thanks to Chris Price and Rebecca Priestley, who spent hours reading drafts of this book and provided valuable feedback. I am also indebted to my supportive cohort of fellow PhD students at the International Institute of Modern Letters for their feedback and to writing friends Helen Lehndorf, Maria McMillan, Helen Rickerby and Airini Beautrais. Damien Wilkins, Bill Manhire, Clare Moleta and Katie Hardwick-Smith also provided much-appreciated support and guidance along the way.

Thanks also to Chris Cochran and Margaret Cochran for facilitating the use of the little cottage in Martinborough, where several of these poems were written; Karen and Keith Stewart for supplying a little writing desk for edits; Allen and Maria Heath for being emotional stalwarts; Fergus Barrowman, Ashleigh Young, Kirsten McDougall, Craig Gamble and Sammy Chorley at VUP for their tireless support of New Zealand poetry.

Some of the work in the creative component has been published in print and online journals; thanks to the editors of: *4th Floor Journal*, *Cordite*, *Hue & Cry*, *JAAM*, *Poetry New Zealand*, *Snorkel*, *Sport*, *Swamp*, and *Turbine*.

This book would not have been written without the Victoria Doctoral Scholarship I received and the support of Victoria University of Wellington, particularly Peter Whiteford.